*The Battle At Home When
Your Soldier's At War*

Judith Bray & Shelley Kaplar

Raider Publishing International

New York   London   Swansea

ISBN: 1-934360-03-1
Published By Raider Publishing International
www.RaiderPublishing.com
New York   London   Swansea

Printed in the United States of America and the United Kingdom
By Lightning Source Ltd.

The Battle At Home When Your Soldiers At War

Judith Bray & Shelley Kaplar

Welcome to hopefully the most interesting and helpful book that you will need to get through your loved one being out in a war zone. Included are a few sites to visit with your computer. We are here to support our soldier any way we can so that the things we do will keep them in a brighter frame of mind. Along the way we have our own war to fight to stay as able as possible to get through all our highs and lows that come to us daily to turn our lives upside down. Haywire emotions that are so extreme we never thought would be within us. How to fill up your time. The pitfalls and the unexpected and various rules and regulations that are bound to pester you. How you can keep in contact. How you can send mail and parcels. This book goes right through to the other end when they finally return.

Why the Authors Wrote this Book

We started out as online strangers in the same situation but from different ends of the playground. It is a mother's view with a son in Iraq, and a girlfriend's view with her boyfriend in Afghanistan.

As a girlfriend this was my first time dealing with anything like this and had never experienced a boyfriend going on tour (let alone having a boyfriend in the military).

As a mum I had known my son always with an army career so I wasn't so fresh to the military.

War makes everything turn on its head. We met from the ebluey chatboard and fast became friends as we both have a zany sense of humour so got on so well, and this is when we became brave. This book came about by the two of us chatting away into the wee small hours of the morning on how to cope and the things to send to our loved ones who had been sent out on 6-month tours. I was looking for more ideas on what to send to my boyfriend, and me as a mum was doing exactly the same but for my son. Jokingly we said we should write a book since there really isn't anything to go by when dealing with all over the map emotions. Why had we not heard anything when we've been sending tons of blueys (airmail letters), emails and eblueys? (eblueys are special e-mails for the military) So many times not knowing if our parcels we've sent have arrived yet and the list continued.

Each section is set up on dealing with different areas of our experiences and other people's experiences too. So depending on who you have out there whether it's a husband, wife, partner, boyfriend, girlfriend, son, daughter, siblings or pals, there is something in here for everyone. Some say it's a bit like a footy match, and my oh my some days the emotional roller coaster is like being thrown right in the middle of a match. So sit back and enjoy, laugh or cry because the one thing that is learnt through all of this is emotions are quite random but daily and the emotional roller coaster is far more intense than any amusement park ride.

There are pieces that are relevant to everyone, and a broad spectrum of ways you can be affected so we have tried to make a true blend. The ways to do practical things. This book gives advice for your emotional trials but remember your soldier feels exactly the same way. Never ever forget that. It's the fact that they have to cope with it in a different way. It's no good for them crying when they are on duty or having tantrums or a reliable fighting force they could not be. So read on and we are sure this is the best thing since sliced bread. Oh to have had such a book as this to help us claw our way through.

Finding Out they are being sent out and Leading up to the Departure Date

Even though we know what we were getting into we still aren't prepared for hearing the words, "I'm being sent to (insert country of your choice) and I leave on this date." The bomb has just been dropped (no pun intended) and it feels like your stomach has hit the floor and your heart has stopped beating. You think well this is their job and someone has to do it. This is what they signed up for and this is what we had to expect with them in the service. A favourite, as my inner voice screamed at the top of it's lungs in my head, OH MY GOD I CAN'T BELIEVE THEY HAVE TO GO!!!! Now the one thing that I found out rather quickly is dates can change at the drop of a hat. First they are leaving on this date then it gets bumped up a few months or weeks, then it gets delayed, and just when you think you've got it all sorted and emotions are back under control they come home to tell you they are leaving next week. This is the time when you are flying around like a mad thing so that your head can take it all in. You feel crushed. What has to be done? What should be done first? Are there priorities? Everything looks at you head on and each seem as important to another. Oh where should you start? Will there be enough time to complete things? The crisis has begun.

For parents it isn't quite the same especially if your son or daughter flew the nest a while ago and what I got was a phone call from my son to tell me all about it (not so hands on). He said oh so proudly that maybe he will be going away. Ha ha some "maybe" as I knew it's a certainty! He was just saying that to give me hope that there could be a chance he was not leaving. That's kids for you, eh? Trying to cushion the blow if possible, as they definitely don't want you collapsing with the phone in your hand or for them to hear you screeching or blubbering. It makes

7

you wonder if their regiment had been told to do the soft approach. In my head I thought, 'oh bless him he is being so sensitive to my feelings on the matter.' The facts of the news then made my hand shake and I nearly dropped the phone and I had to bite my lip so that I wasn't showing upset with a trembling voice. At this point I sat down. I reckoned it was the safer option. I dare not hint of the worry about it because I didn't want him to think I was an emotional jelly. My head buzzed and the first thing that sprung to mind, is what the media had shown on the news or in the paper. Oh hell, he is going to be part of that. Horrendous. This can't be true. Oh to be able to give him huge hugs and kisses as he continued with this mind blowing information. Lots of sloppy comfort came from both sides and then I wondered why he sounded so happy that he is off to Iraq with his pals. Comradeship and pride I suppose.

Huh …. Wow how can the soldiers feel this way but you can't see how worried they truly are. They probably are putting on a brave face. What brave face? I don't think as an after thought that he was trying to kid me. He sounded way too jolly to be pretending and he really was excited to be off to explore the unknown. I don't think it really bothered him at all. That was the impression I got. Here was me just seeing the negative side of things and him seeming like somebody who was going off on a holiday. All a huge fun experience. Off to pastures new and away from the UK to work elsewhere for a change. War seemed to be the last thing on his mind opposite to me with it being in the forefront. He was totally positive about it all. A good thing I suppose or they would be unfit to get on with their job. Don't get me wrong because he knew all the possible dangers and hazards that would be hitting them daily but, I think soldiers are trained from day one when they join up to be as aloof and as fearless as they possibly can be should they ever be needed for awful situations. Inside they truly are as stressed and as scared as you. They know how to cope with it better is the big difference. I think they are so in key with the negative side of their lifestyle that the positive side oozes through and wins every time. The thing that sticks out like a sore thumb through the venture from start to finish is that the hardest reality is to be apart. It envelops you totally. Then coming in a very close second place is the danger that dashes at random in and out of your thoughts. That is not the order of importance. Just the way your brain works. 'Why?' said my son, should the troops feel down when they know they can feel secure and rely and depend on each of their mates. Enormous trust. No doubt so over the top we can't imagine. Then I was told he had written a Will. Something they all have to do. I was named to be the person who gets informed if anything happens to him. I know all about that bit from times he's been away before, but it still hits you when you hear about it.

By this time I was freaking out. Then I was given the part of the war zone he was off to but was assured as soon as they all get there they will all contact with the full address if they do not know it before they leave. Here I think you are meant to be so pleased but you are not. Lots of ordinary casual happy chat somehow got mingled in. Don't ask me why, but it would seem some natural reaction causes this. Eventually the call ended with the fact they all will be safe so don't worry. I was asked to let other members of the family know. In my case too, to keep in regular contact with his partner and child. The phone went down having had drawn out cheerio's. That is a call I can never forget.

Unbelievably traumatised by this with head amass with this sickening reality the whole thing seemed overwhelming. Now I was well and truly stuck with the war at home of coping with the war he was in. Staring at my computer I visualised all the emails now to be sent to him. Then heavens, how do I tell the rest of the family and friends this nasty news without falling apart in the process? He had been to quite a few war zones since joining up and they didn't hit home to me much at all. This hit me harder because it was on the news, daily.

Let me tell you this. Though one tour is never like

another for the soldiers. For loved ones it doesn't get easier with emotions. It just means that you get to know a lot more as to how the routines and pitfalls can occur. The reasons why this or that can happen. That's the only improvement. If you can call it an improvement. Emotions run as high each time. If anyone says differently then they are a liar or as tough as old army boots.

Soldier's Going Away Problems

Now we aren't the only ones on this wonderful emotional roller coaster. Our loved ones are on their own as well, just in a different sort of way. Their random thoughts can include various aspects. Will I come home? Will they still be here when I get back? Will they have found someone else while I've been gone for so long? I don't want them to worry about what I'm doing out there. Will my kids still remember me when I get home? Will they think I have deserted them? Not to mention all the things they have to have in order before they go. Next of kin as to who gets contacted first. A Will to be made.

When my boyfriend told me that this was completed my heart stopped along with everything else that moves. I know somewhere in my intellectual level that I knew that this would have to be done, but to actually hear the words telling you… it put things into a different perspective.

Automatic payment of bills. Cancelling of services that won't be needed while out in the war (cable, and what not). Getting an "Off Road" license for the car. The list of things to be done can be a huge list that they have to deal with one by one so that all is just right. Crossing off each one as it is seen to. Then they can leave with no pressure, thinking once they go, the doubt needn't be there to niggle them that they have forgotten to sort out any single thing. It would be done with barely a thing missed out if any.

Final Rows

Then the rows start, somewhere out of the blue when you least expect it (usually when you've had a really great day together) there it is, blindsiding both of you. Well now you just have to run with it. Who walks away from a really good row when you might as well continue on with it? Topics in this category can include; Don't be daft I'm not going to be out looking for anyone else while you're gone. Of course you're coming back so don't be talking like that. Yes, I'll still be here when you come home. Of course I know how to pay bills so the electricity doesn't get turned off. Of course I'm going to write to you. I am going to write to you tons. Who else would I write to out there? Yes I love you and am going to miss you. But I'm sure you get the idea and are either nodding your head right now or laughing because you've participated in one or all of these rows.

They are Leaving

A few days before they are due to set out, the waterworks start and these just aren't a few tears they are full on flood warnings. The world feels like it's ending, although we are trying to be brave and put up a tough front so as not to stress our loved one anymore than they are already. They are unsure about leaving and what they will encounter over there. So now starts the closet crying. We only try to cry when they aren't looking if in the same room, or gone off to work for the day. We keep repeating our mantra, "I will not cry the day they fly out. I will not cry the day they fly out." When we come to dropping them off we'll at least wait until they can't see us anymore and we unpack the box of tissues from the boot so we'll be able to see as we drive back home through the tears. Once we get back home we start a letter so they have something from home when they get there and to know how much we love them and miss them already even though it's only been one hour since they left, knowing that they'll be chuffed to bits to see that they have a letter waiting for them upon their arrival. Ok, they may not get it for a couple of days but its nice to envision that the moment they reach camp then there it will be.

You may not see them off in which case staring at the clock for hours till time of departure is commonplace. As a mum I was an excellent example of that. Thoughts may come of "Heck, they will be in the air by now." Ha ha ... not "will" but "maybe" is more appropriate, as nothing leaves on time. "TIME" is a big word that everything revolves around from start to finish. Imagination flooded through my mind. I never have been the sort to cry like many people so floods of tears washed my mind instead over and over and over. That was the way it affected me, that is the way I am, a strong outward display. I held back those tears and somehow I tried to look as if I was truly coping. Looks are so very deceptive because the inside gut wrenching is huge. Being unable to cry doesn't help because all is bottled up inside. My make-up didn't run, my face wasn't wet but oh boy did I still need those tissues as I started finding my nose constantly needed a good blow. It either ran profusely so much so the tissues were constantly at my side. My red sore upper lip wasn't inviting to see, and at other times my nose was so blocked breathing could be difficult. My voice came out at a different level so that many times I was far from coherent. Mumbling made my husband give the eyes down and a definite look that made me feel the same as when I was at school and being overawed by a teacher unsatisfied by my work because she did not approve of my standard. Exactly like that. That cheesed off look at me from my husband because he was getting fed up from deciphering half of what I said. I would smile a sweet but forced smile back at him trying to pretend I was fine. Mmmn, what an idiot I seemed to be and the English language was more like some unknown foreign language that I had certainly learned very quickly to speak since my son phoned. Cut to ribbons and falling apart was ghastly despite no sign of tears. What seemed a hard shell or cool hearted and coping person was so far from it. Soft as soft inside and out. Every little weirdness from the norm or my stupid attitude no doubt gave the impression that I may soon be ill enough to need treatment. Hahaha. Ok not quite. My son could never think this was how loving sensible Mum would behave at all. He would be so disappointed at my emotional distress.

The Lack of Communication from the Time that they Leave

If you hear from your loved one just after they arrive then you are considered very lucky. Depending on the camp that they are going to will depend on how soon they can call or email home. You can usually expect to wait anywhere from a few days to a few weeks before you hear anything. In this time frame you will have sent tons of blueys (airmail letters), emails or eblueys letting them know days events. Mainly all the good things that are happening that can make them smile and enjoy. Mundane and important stuff too. Like the washing came out all tinged in pink because silly you put in an item that was red. The kettle broke so you needed to buy a new one. All the things that went wrong just to bug you more.

How come these things always seem to go wrong when it means you have to deal with it? The info that you tripped on a paving slab and ripped your tights! You will say how the kids are doing and their day at school along with the news of the rest of the family. But with nothing in response it gets quite frustrating and the worrying sets in. It is essential you keep sending them mail though because it

13

is an important link to home. Think yourself lucky that you are free here at home to do whatever you want and when you want. You can socialise and you have family and friends so you can cry on their shoulders when you are feeling down. They have no shoulders to cry on have they? That must be so so hard.

When they go off on tour it's not like a normal job of going to a conference where they show up at the Hilton all with "Hi MY Name is" badges on their jackets with an itinerary of the months events knowing that they'll be done by 7pm each evening to retire to their plush rooms or the option of lounging by the pool and call home. Depending on the state of the camp when they get there can make quite a difference. They could be getting into the routine of continuing to set everything up. They may be starting from scratch and setting up a new camp or get lucky and get attached to a camp that is already set up, or the take over of the camp from the regiment that has completed their tour. Even then it can take two weeks to settle the troops and have it up and running the best way for them.

Depending on the number of men and women assigned to this camp will depend on the line ups for computers and phones when it comes time to call home. Often they even have to book a time to use these. Not to mention the usual things they must get used to straight away such as getting over the jet lag for the first two days. Adapting to a complete change in temperature so they can get used to living and working in the intense heat. They have to get to know the full lay out of the camp. There is the settling into their work schedule. These can sometimes be eighteen hour days for them, which can be pretty grueling, wearing all that kit all day or night depending on what shift they have.

It was four weeks before I received my first phone call from my boyfriend and every day, well more like every hour on the hour (who am I kidding) I would be checking my mobile to see if he had rung. I don't have a landline so my phone was with me everywhere I went. There were days I would ring my mates and get them to ring me back just to make sure that it still worked. Or I would stare at it willing it to ring and have it be my boyfriend on the other line (note to self this one doesn't work, it falls into the category of a watched pot never boils). Once I found out the time difference I would then calculate what time it was. I wondered where he was and try to imagine what he'd be doing at that particular moment. This was all done in my down time and I have since found things to do to occupy my time. Absolute craziness I know but with being a first timer I had no idea as to what to expect for phone calls, considering I was used to talking to him all the time.

The first time I had missed his call I was totally gutted and secretly wished that I hadn't been working at the time so I could devote sitting patiently by the phone to be able to hear his voice whenever he was able to call. I figured he would've just left me a message but no. No such luck. I then couldn't figure out why he didn't leave me a message and then my brain started working over time (not a good thing) and I was even more anxious for my mobile to ring again. He finally called back after an extremely painful and what seemed like forever, but was actually two hours. When I had asked why he didn't leave me a message he replied quite nonchalantly "baby, I knew you were busy and I'd just ring you back when I knew I could get a hold of you." Well, if that just didn't sound simple and matter of fact. Much nicer really, than the reasons I had been cooking up in my over active imagination.

The Work they do can Leave Times with no way they can Contact You

They also get sent out on patrol along with other various operations. They go off on two-week exercises and they aren't allowed to tell us when they are doing this or where they are going. They are only allowed to call us when they get back. So we must get used to infrequent

15

contact even once their schedule supposedly "normalises" and they find a time that works to call home. Do try to calm down and don't get too flustered. Then sometimes we get nothing. Panic starts setting in and we become newsaholics… watching, listening to any and all news that we can get our hands on because we haven't heard anything. Once again we start repeating another mantra "they are safe just busy, they are safe just busy, they are safe just busy," while keeping in mind no news is good news.

A good rule of thumb is limit the news watching or stop all together because developing an ulcer while they are gone does neither one of you any good. Highly recommended is to channel hop the moment the news comes on. A great deal of it is either the same horror reported over and over for days. Who wants to be upset with it being chewed over just so the media can wave their flag and spread it out just for their own gain?

Shown are films of soldiers out on patrol in the streets. Those make your imagination go wild, knowing that your soldier could be doing that or other jobs in various shapes and forms depending on who they are. A lot of the news is political comment on why we went to war in the first place and continuing their plans as to what the troops should do next. Many reports about their vehicles, clothing or weapons being less adequate than they should be. You have to admit that such talk will make you angry and heartbroken with your loved one bang in the middle of it. Get it well and truly glued in your mind with superglue that "No news is Good news." Never forget that at any time. It's easy to say but oh so hard to do. We are only human. If you really can manage to cancel the newspapers then that is a huge bonus. However again we stress for you to always keep in mind that nothing is given to the media before the contact person is told. If something did happen we would know quite quickly as the military doesn't build up the suspense on bad news. If you have seen something awful via the media then you know that the contacts have already had that sorry news. The appropriate person is informed within two hours of a bad incident.

You are always going to be jumped on by friends saying, "What do you think about "such and such" that the latest media reports are saying?" First of all, you don't want to know something has happened as that's going to break you up. You oh so wish they hadn't said. Now you are dashing about madly to find out what has gone on. That can be such a panic for you. Believe me people are going to tell you things and also ask what area your soldier is based because it happened at "such and such" a place. They mean well by trying to get involved and be interested in the situation so that is good to know. They really do care even though at the time you can't see this. It seems they cannot gauge on what you want to hear and what you prefer not to.

My mum would continue to ask every time she heard something on the news, "Does he really have to be there?" or "Can't he just come home?" Although I love my mum to bits, to have to always hear that every time I talked to her was difficult. I had to keep reassuring her that he was fine and had just talked to him, or would hear from him as soon as he could ring me. She has this great idea that they can just decide that they don't want to go, or just get to come home whenever they want to, bless her. I had to keep reminding her that this wasn't a job that you could just call in sick for or submit a doctor's note and then he wouldn't have to go. But the one thing that did help me with having to calm my mum's fears was it helped to reinforce my own calmness that everything was going to be okay and he'd be home soon.

Lines Down

It is a term used when all phones and computers are disabled. A safety feature usually used if the camp is on a high alert. It could be because some terrible incident has happened or there is real turmoil. These lines can sometimes be down for many days. Chat will be rife which will send your emotions going into speed mode. Is the regiment ok? My loved one is camped there or near there. Extreme visions and thoughts are gripping you. Again this is where the mantra comes in, "No news is Good news, No news is Good news." They will be phoning to let you know that they are safe as soon as they can get word out. Absolutely no short cuts to this ruling. It's the not knowing and trying to comprehend that rips you to bits. After it has happened to you a few times you will get more used to it. You will understand it more.

The Phone Call

When you get your phone calls there will be tears of excitement and worry and twenty minutes goes by very quickly. Every little word is a treasure no matter what you happily and lovingly chat about. You just wish the calls could go on and on but, they can't. However you do get used to it and the conversations turn out to be quite normal, just short. You learn to push as many things into the chat as possible. Enjoy it all from start to finish and fill it with happy things that you have been itching to tell them.

They get twenty free minutes a week on phone cards so they can call home, although we've heard rumours that this has been changed to thirty free minutes a week. This generous gift from the army is less than three minutes per day! You can top up their phone card as well so it gives them more time to talk, by calling 01438 28 2121 and you will need their phone card number along with their rank and name. Lets face it we are sure you will want longer phone calls than three minutes per day.

There will be times that the phone calls can last anywhere from two minutes to the full twenty minutes. This depends on the connection and if the signal gets dropped. My boyfriend would sometimes give me the warning that his credit was about to end to give me the heads up, in case we got cut off. Usually we would talk until the call would end on its own that way we wouldn't have to say good-bye (or my favourite since I hate to say good-bye, see ya later) though making very sure we got our "I love you's" and "I miss you's" into the conversation so the call wouldn't end without each other hearing those words. Also through the company that the military uses for phone cards they can send and receive texts, along with sending emails and receiving replies. This was such a great bonus.

Some makes of mobile phones do not work out in certain countries and so be sure that the phone they take is suitable. Heck, every good thing has a down side to equal it, which is typical. No worries though, because they can buy phones in some places where they are based. It is changing to whether their personal phones may be banned altogether as the army reckon they are a big risk. We will just have to see what their decision on that is.

Phone Calls Care

When they phone there are certain things that can't be said over the lines just in case any of the baddies are picking up the conversation. Yes, there is technology out there for them to do it. Don't be distressed if the landline phone gets cut off mid call because each phone does this as necessary. This monitoring can be a proverbial pain in the butt. However, that is for safety reasons so one thing to smile about is that here is another way our troops are cared for. Do be careful what you say on mobiles as the enemy has methods to access them too. Do not speak of Army dates or chat about events that have happened or are going to happen. No talk about how the forces are coping with something or plans they may be considering. Your soldier took an oath when they joined up to restrict a great deal of information so don't make it hard for them by trying to draw it out. When it comes to dates for them to return home they have to be put in a letter or email as to not endanger them or the rest of the troop.

Phoning Cuddles

There will be times when they phone and they seem a bit down or detached from the conversation. This is because they miss us and are probably having a bad day or week of things out there. They've called to hear our voice to pick up their spirits and to remind them that yes, we do love them and miss them as much as they do us. They haven't called to torment us with feelings of insecurity. They've called because being the great conveyers of emotions that they need a cuddle from the one that they love and the phone call is the only way that it can happen.

A far cry from the real thing, but a cuddle nonetheless to make everything a little bit more okay. Like us they too experience the rides on the emotional roller coaster, but are trained to handle it differently. However hearing each other's voices for as long as the conversation lasts puts a smile like there's no tomorrow on both of your faces.

I Want to Send a Parcel. Whatever Will I Put in it?

The information for the parcels are the ones that worry you greatly as you think they must be difficult to send off first time or every time. It makes you feel "Wherever do I start?" Don't fret as after the first one you'll be an expert and wonder why you ever thought it could be complex. The moment they have left you wonder if they have packed this that or the other. How will they cope without a certain item? So you are determined you will send them vital necessities "just in case" that somehow they were left off their list. If they already have it, then they can save it for later. Also you want to include little extras and treats to make them smile. So here are many suggestions to keep you going throughout their time away. Things to send plus some things not allowed.

Here's a list of items that make great ideas for a parcel:

White hanky with lipstick kisses (yours) all over it so they can have your kisses close to their heart. You can also spray a bit of your perfume on it as well.

Crisps and snack items that they usually munch on at home.

Powdered drink mixes. You can order some online either from ebay, or from www.fpsplus.com who provide an energy drink for athletes. Soldiers have to drink between 10-15 litres of bottled water per day to prevent dehydration and so much can be very bland so these additions make it healthier and tastier.

Sun cream if they are somewhere hot and preferably over a factor 15. They want a tan but don't want to be sore and in agony.

Chap stick with a SPF in it.

Individually wrapped mints for their pockets when they are out on patrol. Polo mints are a popular favourite.

Individually packaged wet naps as a refresher for them.

Baby wipes (the non-perfumed ones.) They are so soothing and an absolute boon because sand gets everywhere. In every little crevice it can find. These wipes are so cooling. A must.

Small hand held fans with water mister to deal with the heat.

Their favourite type of tea.

Tons of pictures of you specially orientated with family, friends, and pets or even house and garden. Just whatever you think will be loved.

Plaster imprints of kids feet or hands for new fathers.

Hand and footprints using water paint on paper or card. It can be hard to do if baby curls up toes or fingers. Try to send different coloured ones in each parcel.

Paintings done by the children.

Little teddy bears ... sounds silly but soldiers think they are cute especially with little messages on their tums. They have a hard job to do but the soldiers are big softies inside and it's a special comfort link.

If sending chocolate to somewhere hot then you might want to put it in the freezer for two weeks prior to sending and then wrap it in bubble wrap. Then put it in a zip lock bag so if it does melt it doesn't get all over everything else in the parcel. The bubble wrap will act as an insulator so it doesn't melt. The same goes for any cookies that you want to send but you just have to wrap the container of frozen cookies not each individual one. It is handy to put a cool bag in... just tell them to post it back!! Make sure the chocolate is in a separate bag from the rest of the items in the parcels or the whole parcel can arrive with a huge sticky melted mush inside, gunge cannot describe it. Yucky!! As for them eating it then it has a tendency to melt in their hands before it gets to the mouth so they will need to eat it quickly, which I'm sure will not be a problem!!

Magazines or local newspapers. Sports results or information on their favourite footy team.

Anything to do with their general interests.

Puzzle books.

Mugs.... sensible, silly or a wee bit naughty!

Underwear... Practical or totally impractical but not so many that they overflow with them. Again it comes down to space or the need for them. Locker space is not huge so keep that in mind.

T-shirts. You could get a photo of you printed on it.

Hand held tape recorder with tapes of personalized messages from your loved ones and from you or the kids.

For those with a camcorder you can copy home movies of the kids to DVD for them so they can watch them on the computer or send along a personal DVD player with some of their favourite movies. This also works for recording first days at school, parties, baby's first steps or any other "what not" so it will feel like they are there with you.

CDs of the music they enjoy. Mini CD players means they can lay back on their beds and look like a goon with their headphones.

Toiletries, shower gel, soap, after-shave, cologne, and deodorants. Shaving soap. Perfume and make up for the young ladies, because I can't see the chaps wanting it. Any pongy stuff is a must to make their very sweaty selves smell sweeter ha ha ha.

Prezzies the kids have chosen are excellent. Makes the kids feel they are involved with the contents so that's a bonus.

Paraphernalia for any coming up holiday, i.e.: Birthdays, anniversaries. At Christmas then include tinsel, stockings and Santa hats. Love hearts. Easter eggs, if it's not too hot, and sweets. If you send Christmas crackers you should remove the explosive tabs. It sounds drastic and totally idiotic but they are illegal.

Things You Can't Send

Anything aerosol or carbonated/fizzy drinks. The pressure within the cargo area of the planes is unstable and will cause them to explode. It is a hazard to the plane and you don't want to ruin other people's mail too.

Razor blades or any other type of sharp object.

Alcohol or porn. Being caught will result in a fine, or fine plus watching the items getting destroyed. This includes chocolates with liqueurs in them. Fines can range from one hundred to one thousand quid. It's certainly not worth the risk. Please realise the Customs police are strict and impose these illegalities. Customs have the right to inspect parcels at random whenever they want to.

Meats are a definite no! They are not fit to send and no airports round the world accept it. Plus it is a huge culture shock if they are found in some countries with certain religions.

No flammable fluids, such as lighter fuel.

Those are just a few ideas to get you started and once you send one parcel then the ideas just keep coming. You will spot things when you are out shopping that could be a "something" that they may like to get. So be sure to notice these.

Don't be too distressed because there is always a shop on the camp for them to buy food and many other things. There is not so much of a selection of branded goods such as toiletries and they may prefer a brand of something that isn't stocked. Also, they prefer to get things from home. A parcel from you and the fun they have delving into it to see what you have sent, is a dream. It's totally different than them going to the camp shop for basics. Do not send them main foods such as tins of things, it's a waste of space and adds extra weight to the parcel. Don't send them clothes apart from underwear. It has to be stressed that they have little room to put things.

How to Send a Parcel

Each parcel must not weigh more than 2kg so be sure you have weighed it correctly as you don't want to turn up at the post office and have to open it to take something out of your so beautifully, safely and securely wrapped parcel, only for it now to be ruined. It is so upsetting in many ways. It can be heart breaking. Tears fall and those tissues are needed once again. Make-up running as well as steam coming out of your ears is not a pretty sight.

Be sure to list the contents on the back or side of the parcel. There is no need to be precise. Reading material, smelly stuff/toiletries or whatever name comes to mind that describes each. You must correctly address it including name rank and number and put BFPO in big letters. BFPO number (British Forces Post Office) is an army postal code for the area where the camp is. Put your own address on the back so that the parcel can be returned to you if it gets lost or if you have incorrectly addressed it. Parcels have to be paid for except during the month up to Christmas when it's free. Whoopee. The post office will know the dates for freepost.

All the BFPO parcels get sent by forces' planes. Check to make sure with your local post office for any extra details should you need them. However, it is all very straight forward. Post it at your post office and jump up and down with delight when you are told it's got there. All the fun of putting the contents together and the delight that it's arrived and pictures go through your mind to your soldier opening it and going "Oh wow this is ace. I am loved, loved and loved." Only you know what other things that may be said. Mmmmn, that's for you to know hahaha as to the reaction. For sure it will cause degrees of delight. Immeasurable.

If you are living outside of the UK then you'll need to post the parcel to your British soldiers UK military address and then it will be forwarded on from there.

What Parcels Can Do

All parcels lift every soldier's spirits absolutely to unbelievable heights. I am quite sure that anything sent will be treasured, eaten (not too fast, as they want to, so they can make it last as long as possible) things worn, smiled at and those causing a sentimental rush with special memories of home and family. Such love pours out from that parcel. It isn't just the contents but knowing that you wrapped the parcel. Every item included was chosen by you and specially thought about. The fact that you went around the shops looking for the things they really will enjoy and the more fun things that make them laugh their heads off. The things that you know are a must for them regarding practical goods needed. Sweets and snacks to make them lick their lips. Much love is exuded from there with whatever it may be. Tears of happiness roll down their cheeks from things to do with you. There will be happy tears for the kids and things done by them. The amazing artwork they do. Items that are chosen especially by the children. These have been picked for their mum or dad. How warm is that. Photos of their loved ones closest to them tug at their heartstrings. They like to lie back on their beds and look through them making their smiles get wider. Time and time again you will be making up parcels to send because they absolutely adore getting them. There is no doubt about that. You can see how special that parcel is. Wooohoooo, a real high to put them on top of their barracks.

Christmas was such a laugh when they got sent tinsel to hang round their beds. Little mini fibre optic trees just seven inches tall to put on a cupboard or wherever was best for such an item. Reindeer and other very small soft toys. It was amazing how many people sent Santa hats. How hilarious would soldiers look wearing them with their uniform? Mmmm, imagine that!! Hard to envisage I expect. It could look threatening to the enemy. A Christmas stocking to hang on the end of their bed with mini gifts in. Such variety. Things called Santa Keys to hang up. How else would Santa get in with there being no chimney? We have been told that the items wrapped with Christmas wrapping paper are kept unopened without trying to nose in... ok maybe a few sneaky peeks or "feels" to try and guess what the present is. They wanted to be opening them with their friends and workmates and go "wow" altogether. Cool, with such resilience, to actually wait. I had to laugh imagining our soldiers pulling the crackers minus the tab so they had to say "bang" to give a similar effect. It is equivalent to seeing a child saying "brrm brrm" driving their imaginary car.

So send those parcels, which so obviously are a must. They are so important. You never know you may receive something like flowers, chocolates and other presents from them sometimes. That really does make you cry with happy tears so out will come your box of tissues again and it is guaranteed you will be telling everyone that you have got something. Getting anything is a big occasion that everyone should know about. Will you shout it from the rooftops? Of course you will.

Letters, As Many As You Can

Blueys are forces airmail letters. No postage is required for them and there is no need to buy them either. Ask for a handful of them from your post office so you have them at hand to write when that feeling comes upon you (like any hour, day or night). Admittedly, some post offices have real dragons who run it and are a true pain. They reckon they know it all and often they don't. Be assured that they must give you blueys and also emphasise that no stamp is required for sure, should the dragons say to the contrary.

Write as many as possible. Say anything and everything to make them feel closer to home. Tell of the good things that happen. Include the very ordinary everyday things that go on. Any important things, loving things, fun things, and include the not so good things that have happened. The whole spectrum of life as to how it really is.

Put in all of the local gossip to keep them up to date. They will want to hear it all. Now lets not get silly and decide not to tell of occasions you have gone to, or parties, or trips you have done all because you think they may be jealous you are enjoying yourself at times. They love to know you are having a good time, so no holding back on that. When I say all I mean all. Never miss out things just because you think your soldier only wants to hear about the happy stuff. It won't ring true if things are held back. Obviously the bluey has to be as cheery and loving as you can make it. To outweigh any "down" sides that hopefully are very rare occasions or fingers crossed are never, then keep any "down" things very short and don't harp on them. Have a few moans. You would when you are together. They are permitted. These letters are for brilliant things not bad. These blueys mean so much plus seeing the words in your own sweet handwriting. Even if it is a scrawl and your writing isn't too fabulous then so what. You have put pen to paper. Believe me, those letters will be kept with care to be read again and again. Most mail will probably be stashed under their pillow so they can more than likely nod off reading them and dream sweet dreams of home. Admittedly blueys are not as fast as using the computer but if you write plenty they get a good regular flow of mail to boost them up.

Instant Messenger

This is an ideal way to keep in touch. It is probably one of the nearest to being as close and interactive as possible. Yack away to your heart's content. Ok, it's not "never ending" but it's a boon. If you don't have your own computer, use a friend's. It will be one of the best things you can do. Just realise that a soldier's shift will determine when they can use the computer and if lots of people intend to use it then there can be various lengths of waiting time. Fingers crossed there are times when they can have use of it with nobody else wanting it at the same time. Work out time zones, as it may mean you will be on it at some unearthly hour through the night. Get an alarm clock set or stay up till the early hours to catch them. It's not ideal if you are getting little sleep, anyway. Nothing is simple or straightforward. Everything is worth waiting for at any time. I am sure you would agree on that.

My boyfriend and I were able to instant message each other, which was great and our conversations could last anywhere from five to twenty minutes. Although we could get a good run in when he would go and get back in the queue so we could continue our conversation. There was one day that we were online for a whole hour (someone was a little over the moon then, not mentioning any names) with four short breaks in between, due to the queue's not being all that long. Sometimes the transmitting time was slow in getting and receiving the messages, which although frustrating, was also good for a giggle because I was certain our typing wasn't that slow compared with our previous conversations.

Why Is The Mail Apparently Not Getting There?

There are also times, for whatever reason we really aren't too sure, that they aren't getting the eblueys or blueys we've been sending, as fast as they should. This can be because the printer isn't working too well for some unknown reason at the printing station or the mail is backlogged at either end. It might be because it isn't at the safest of times to deliver to the camps. Then all of a sudden they get hit with a ton of mail from you and it takes them days to read through it all. You can be sure they are breathing a sigh of relief that we haven't forgotten them.

The same goes for our end when they send out blueys or cards. We know that they have sent us something so we are anxiously awaiting its arrival, when once we've estimated how long it should take to get to us and unfortunately it hasn't arrived yet. We then start to anticipate the postman's arrival and cursing him silently if he walks past the house without a second glance. We then do a double check on the letterbox to see if maybe he found the letter at the bottom of his bag and had to return past our house to drop it off. We contemplate ringing up the post office to see if our postman has taken a vacation and no new postman was assigned to the route. Yes this has crossed my mind once or twice! But again, for the mail going out from the country that they are in, all depends on when the cargo plane is ready and can take off or land safely.

Boxhappy.com

Are you a bit stuck for other ideas for your parcels? Then perhaps your problem is solved. You can send parcels for all occasions, both special and ordinary, via the net with Boxhappy. Look at Boxhappy because they have countless choices. It's a site that sends off to your loved one the parcel of your choice. Have a look at this option and you will see what I mean. A site especially for you and your soldier to use, so you can send gifts or parcels to one another, all beautifully wrapped with a card inside. Decide for yourself if Boxhappy is something you might want to use. There is no harm in peeping. On the ebluey site next to your soldiers name in your address book, you will see a little file picture to click upon and that will take you to the Boxhappy site.

The Ebluey Site

Sending an ebluey, which is the real reason for the site, is a way to send a special e-mail, which stays confidential. The army receives what you send and prints it out in letterform and a machine seals it automatically. Nobody reads it at any stage. They give it to the soldier no matter where they are. Even if they are out in the field or off camp it will be taken to them. Hopefully it is delivered within 24 to 36 hrs. Sometimes it can be just a matter of hours if they are extremely lucky. If you wish, you can send a photo ebluey. This is the facility to have a photograph printed on to the ebluey. How cool is that?

Again don't worry if sometimes it takes longer. "Time" which you have noticed by now is not to be relied upon and is approximate.

The ebluey site is excellent to get support from other people in the same boat as you. You will soon learn that you are not the only one with weird emotional problems. It is ideal to swap information between other loved ones upon its message board. Ask questions about things you want to know. Happy messages and chit chat are recommended as scare mongering is highly panicking. You don't want to panic people any more than you want people to panic you.

Personal Email addresses are permitted. If you put yours on the board then some people may send you an email or likewise you send an email to someone on there. Possibly a friendship will be forged so that you can both be more supportive to each other so that you won't feel alone.

What Will Be Deleted From Messages Posted On Military Message Boards?

All the boards are monitored so that swearing, dates of military events and urls will just show up as xxxxx in their place. Those things are totally unnecessary for you to put in. Be respectful and don't use blaspheme. These safety precautions are to help to keep our troops safe as to where and when they will be coming and going. Our enemys read these boards in the hope that information might be dropped and that they could use to their advantage.

Support the Troops Messages

On another section of this site you can post messages to your loved one over there. A different place where you can send your soldier love. At some camps "The Support the Troops" page gets printed out for every soldier to check to see if they have a message posted from home. It's fun to read the other messages posted. Who isn't nosey? Very few of us. Admit it you can't resist to read tons of them out of interest, plus it is also comforting to know that there are other people out there that feel the same way that we do and show love to their soldier as much as we want to show ours.

Home Page of Ebluey Site for Teddy Bears

Here you will find an advert for different types of small teddy bears in three types actually. Click on the photo of the type of bear you want and it will show you the many examples of them. All are extremely cute. There is the military teddy bear dressed in uniforms of many different regiments. Even if you don't get one they are nice to browse through and make you smile. You might get one for yourself or for any children so they can imagine mum or dad in uniform. A few are even sent out to the soldier. I can't guarantee this to be a very good idea. They would probably be ragged for such an item. It certainly seems it's maybe a weird thing to do.

Sometimes, some people need eccentric things from home if that's their choice. It's not in the same category in the way they all love silly Santa items and very miniscule soft toys at Christmas time. Then lots of the soldiers get them so they are not the odd one out. These teddy bears can be bought anytime through the year though. Meant for the family at home, not really for the soldier. There are two other styles of teddy bear but they are for you to look through and decide which type is best. Hey, I can't tell you everything, or phew this book would be endless.

On this home page there is a shop advertised with all types of wonderful things. Varying prices from cheap medium or downright expensive. So you do have a choice to fit your pocket. It's fun to search through them all even if the majority of people will find that the way expensive ones will make you suck your teeth and wonder how anyone can afford the very costly "out of your reach" ones. I know it made me ponder over it. You too can dream the "what if I could afford those" type of dream !!

Forces Radio Station

There is the BFBS (British Forces Broadcasting Service) that you can post dedications for birthdays, anniversaries, or for absolutely anything for any time. These will be read on the specified date of your choice, or you can choose any day, and it will be read during regular broadcasting. Just another way to express your love and to show your loved one how much they are missed. Although a word of caution here as well, even though they are glowing inside with knowing why it was sent a miniscule few can also experience a feeling almost like dread when they are ragged by others who are jealous and haven't had anything posted. So they may vent their anger that this was not such a good idea. Again this is where their emotional roller coaster comes in, as they want to show a tough and resilient exterior to their mates and they hear over the radio your feelings. Sloppy luvvy dovey ones then shoot their macho theory all to bits (in their mind only). However once the initial shock wears off and the leg pulling settles down they are all warm and buzzing inside that you took the time and wanted to show anyone and everyone how much you are proud of them and what they mean to you. This makes them feel special.

These can be a great boost but mainly fun with people just like you. Ones who know how you are feeling. You will probably make many friends in the variety of types of chat rooms with your natter. Some of you may end up emailing or talking to them on instant messenger. Just in the way us authors did. Wasn't that a brilliant meeting for us? Without our meeting, this book would never have got written and you wouldn't be holding it in your hands now. You can be supportive to others as well as have others be supportive to you. While in the chat rooms or on message boards never give out your soldier's full name or rank. This is definitely a very stupid thing to do. Use Christian names or just call them by the relative or friend they are. Boyfriend, girlfriend, partner, husband, wife, son, daughter or pal. Whatever you feel suits best. Keep in mind about not getting panicky if somebody tells you something has happened as nine times out of ten they are exaggerated or half-truths and your imagination goes bananas. Use those chats to cheer you up. Find out tips on how to do certain things and different ways different people handle situations. It's all a big help. You will probably know things others don't know so you can be as equally informative. Especially, with you having this book! Using those rooms can be a big bonus. I suggest if you go to the ebluey site then just leave a note on the message board asking if anyone knows of any specific chat rooms to go to then please can they send you a message. I am sure you will get to hear of several ones that are recommended. It is all part of the fun of getting to find out. Look through to see if any suggested can fit your need the best.

I visited   www.yellowribbon.org.uk   which is a very pleasant and friendly place.

There are the Families of UK Forces in Iraq. FamiliesofUKForcesinIraq@groups.msn.com Another friendly site.

For military info go to www.mod.co.uk

You are in a brand new type of world and learning things daily to get you through this sticky period as best as you can. So search and enquire to spread yourself about.

You may already have your own chat room in which case it might be an idea to invite people to it so they can use it 24/7 if at all possible. It's exactly what this mum did and it was brilliant. I have run my own ordinary chat room for years and when I realised there was a need for people to have a good chinwag any hour of the day or night I gave out my e-address on an ebluey message board. People could contact me to get my room link. So this was handy to be used. Likewise you could do the same. If you don't have a chat room, then think about setting one up. It's amazing what fun they can be for a "round the coffee table" type of chat. Miles of smiles. Something to look forward to every day.

Rumours, Rumours, Rumours

For some strange reason we tend to complicate how we are already feeling without adding rumours into the mix. You will read things on the Message boards of all military sites and in chat rooms of assumed situations. You will hear things from your soldier's mates that are still around if you live near or on the camp they are based back at home.

All these upsetting thoughts of random input contribute to making you doubt the man or woman that you love and have had no problems trusting however many years or months you've been together. You are the only one who knows the person you've fallen in love with and have been with better than anyone else. You know their ability at managing things. So unless there's 200% proof that something's amiss then don't believe a word you hear or read about as to what could be going on or what is going on with someone else's situation. Just because other people have problems doesn't mean that you will experience the same. Our stress level is high enough worrying about their safety that we don't need to complicate matters.

Am I Nuts or Am I Nuts ?

So here you are, desperately trying to cope to the best of your ability. Things seem to get stuck in your way at every turn. Those relatives and friends you were sure would be supportive, don't seem to understand fully. They try to sympathise with you when you start crying for what they think is no apparent reason, throughout the day, night or when the news comes on and the mention of the country where your loved one is. Oh dear, now what? Friends and relatives are brilliant in lots of ways to be there with their shoulders for you to cry on and give you loads of hugs.

However, there is an enormous hole that they cannot fill or understand in the way you thought they would. Compare it to a person trying to comfort someone with a broken limb. The plaster cast can be seen clearly enough but unless the comforter has also had the same injury there is no way to understand or imagine the sort of pain that the break underneath causes. It is exactly the same with you in this situation of your beloved away. The desperate pain and torment you feel cannot be realised by anyone but you. You wonder if you are being totally nuts with such high emotions that spring upon you just any time at all. The loneliness. The feeling of emptiness, even when others are around you. Your temper often frays and the feelings of anger that will take control whenever they haphazardly choose, and then you feel guilty for being so cross. It's normal. So no guilt trips on that. Crying, anger, depression, and sobbing happens so much someone is bound to tell you to stop being so silly and calm down... like you can turn it off like a tap. Just try to not take it to heart for what may seem an insensitive attitude by your family and friends. They just "don't know." They can't fully understand. That broken limb syndrome is what it is. They can't feel your hurt.

People just do not realise that it's always going to make you feel totally ripped to bits from start to finish of the tour. They assume that after a week or two the hurt will magically disappear. Wear off. It doesn't does it? People may be patronising and keep on telling you not to worry as there is nothing going to go wrong. As if such shallow talk could help. Oh how you want to go "grrrrr" at all this falseness. It seems like normality will never exist again. That is why the only thing to make it easier is to reduce your spare time as much as you can. Knowing this as the ticks on your calendar get to be more then so each day gets you closer to the return. When your calendar starts to look on the tatty side you know you are getting through all of this.

Fill Up Your Time

So what can be done to get you through? This is a difficult subject to touch upon because everyone needs to hook on to what works best for them. Be sure that you fill up your time as much as possible as free time becomes thinking time where your mind departs in so many directions resulting in the use of those tissues. Looking a mess seems to be the fashion with red eyes, blotchy face, and many other not so nice things, but again this is a result from worrying and who really looks forward to developing an ulcer? Ok there will be loads and loads of times like that but being engrossed in something can reduce it a little bit. Here are some ideas that maybe you could do.

Read, but stay away from books on war subjects.

Watch TV and videos but remember to stay away from the news.

Play computer games.

Take cooking classes.

Dancing classes, these are good fun if you get a bunch of girls together.

Do puzzle books.

Take up a hobby. Go to a craft shop and choose something to do. Probably it won't be a brilliant result and your painting by numbers or making models may look an ace mess. It doesn't matter. If it gives you something that fills up your time and keeps you busy then that is perfect.

Do jigsaws ... not over big or impossible ones or you will get so mad with it you will only have to pick up the pieces from round the room.

Start a course at college for something you always wanted to do but never got round to doing.

Learn to take really good photos so that you can send better ones to your soldier. (As if he or she really cares what they are like! Even with heads slightly chopped off.)

Go to a gym or take up jogging.

Yoga classes. You are so twisted with worries it must help you to cope with all knotty problems, plus they'll be well impressed that you are extra bendy when they get back home!!

You name it. You do what you fancy and get fun doing it.

I Really Want To Surprise Him Or Her With D.I.Y.

Ok forget the luvvy dovey stuff as that goes without saying! What may make him or her gob smacked is by doing something to the house. DECORATE. A frightening thought that you never considered but there always has to be a first time for everyone at having a go at anything. You will know from previous chats as to how your soldier and you have always wished that certain things needed to be done around the house or in the garden, but neither of you have ever got around to doing it. This is your chance to make those wishes come true. Get some paint and do one or two rooms. Just don't spill it on the carpet or furniture as that will not have been one of the things on the wish list. Ask a friend for guidance to show you the basics on how to paint if you have never done it before. Then you are ready to get it done. If you are really into decorating then wallpaper too. You will get terrific satisfaction from doing it as well as an immense buzz from the result. How cool will that be as a welcome home present? Plus, in doing this it will fill up a big part of your very not needed thinking time. So thumbs up all around! Get stuck into it if you dare!!

Other D.I.Y jobs you might consider having a go at. The thought of doing these things may seem impossible but until you try you will never know if you can. Once again there is bound to be somebody you know to advise you. It's just a case of you doing your best. Be brave and have a go. If it's a total failure does it really matter?

Before your chap comes back try and experiment with your hair. Try it in different shades or colours until you find the one that looks best. Perhaps have it different styles till you find the one that maybe looks the prettiest and sexiest. After all, you don't want to look a wreck when you welcome your soldier home. Then a couple of days or the day before your soldier returns get it done so you can wow him. Maybe if you love well manicured nails spend time to get them sorted too. Work on them so they are perfect and possibly try nail gems on them as mentioned in the "planning for something to do the next day" section.

After all you have months to try and get them tiptop. Get various types of make-up to try out until you find which makes you look the most adorable. Perhaps go out and get a new outfit to be stunning. You could start a new diet or exercise plan? They won't be able to distract or criticise you, when you find it difficult and moan as you try to lose a few unwanted pounds? Geeeeeez, he is going to be over the moon to see you!

Enjoy Things And Accept Things

Enjoy every bit of contact you get back. Be oh so happy with every good thing that comes your way. Accept that waking in the night, inability to sleep and loss of appetite is all part of the rich yucky pattern. You can handle it a bit to be sure. That negative side must be pushed as far as you can to the back of your mind. Way, way back so that it is as minimal as possible. All in all life is going to contain a mass of ups, downs, and nasty mood swings. Great fun... NOT.

Shrink the bad things as much as possible and put it in a mental chest in your head. Admittedly the chest has no key so it isn't always closed but at least have a go and hope that it doesn't fling open as often. You can find the "ups" rather than the "downs" if you search for them. A case of searching in the right places!! However, positive jolly thinking can take the edge off a lot of those "downs."

Doing happy things makes you happier in yourself. This is the way to survive through this chunk of time that you unfortunately are stuck with. You can smile as well as frown. You will be much stronger and more confident. Only you can create it for it won't come about if you mope and don't try. Your soldier would want you to do your very best. At least the days move forward and our countdown decreases. That calendar is showing its age as we get closer to the day they get back home.

I must admit for the most part I was finding ways to deal with my boyfriend being out there, at first I had started using the idea of he's just off on exercise. The only thing that threw a wrench into this plan was the news, so once I stopped watching the news all the time I was able to settle into the thought of him on exercise, even if it was lasting six months. Although once we hit the halfway mark of his tour I did get brave and accepted the fact that he was in a war zone and made sure I kept myself busy with new hobbies and interests till his return. At least test out anything that your mind brings forth. Some may work well, others go down like a lead balloon. Trial and error all the time to discover the handy ways that can help you, for it is essential.

There were definitely times I would miss my boyfriend more than I already did and those were usually weekends, at a movie with my mates, or rainy days where I could just hang out on the sofa with a movie and a comfy blanket. I would be wishing he was here with me to enjoy the movie with or cuddle on the sofa. However it was these moments that I started planning his homecoming and what events would take place and all the planning and preparations to go with it.

Nights seem to be the worst when you lay back in bed and your mind keeps going over and over about things so that your head is so abuzz you just can't fall asleep. Upsetting thoughts just don't help and getting little sleep is not recommended. Try reading a book or doing puzzles to wear you out. If you must think, then plan to do something for the following day. Even if it's to go to the shops and buy something specific. Perhaps get some nail varnish so that you can spend time doing your nails, tomorrow. One thing to do that is very fiddly indeed and time consuming is doing nail art. You can get these little kits of gems cheaply at most make-up sections of supermarkets. The box has about 175 gems of various colours shapes and sizes. Believe me you will get hooked on it. Experiment making different patterns.

Plan to do anything so that you have something to look forward to. Think of something to put in the next parcel. Something that means you have an aim to focus on. Every night when you can't nod off then think again of just one thing you will do for definite tomorrow. Don't try to think of lots of things just one per night. Then be absolutely sure you follow through with whatever you have planned. It is the following through with your plan that completes your aim.

WOOOOOHOOOO I GOT MY FIRST......

Now this could be your first bluey, email, or phone call, and once again the emotional rollercoaster moves on into the gate for departure. There's excitement because you are holding in your very own hands the bluey that was delivered in the post or the reading of an email you found when you checked your inbox. The excitement when you're reading it mixed with floods of tears. Out comes that box of tissues. It may take you longer to read since there's no one to put up a brave face for. You are having at last the dream you have been waiting for which seems to have been an "oh too much longer wait" to get a response from them. The very first phone call with the sound of your soldier's voice that you haven't heard since they left to go on tour. Your blood pressure rises like it has never risen before. You are overjoyed and both of you are clinging onto every single word the other has spoken. Your heart pounds. You are over the moon and want to shout from the rooftops. You feel like you're floating through the air because you've just received your very first contact. It's the best feeling in the world knowing that they are safe and are missing you as much as you are missing them. Neither of you can wait to be back home together. I've received countless emails and blueys and although I've managed to stop crying after the first three that were sent I still get a lump in my throat each and every time I read a new one. As for phone calls I no longer cry after each one (this stopped by call number four), but I looked forward to when I got to hear my boyfriend's voice again no matter how long the conversation will get to last.

As a Mum I got emails. They were brilliant even if they were just a few sentences long. My son's lengthy ones went to his partner, which is understandable. It only takes a couple of lines to put you on cloud nine. I don't think his partner would have been so understanding if hers were as short as mine. In fact I reckon she would have been a mix of being heartbroken and fuming mad at the same time. Very confusing. A Mum, even one who has cut the apron strings, always considers her son or daughter as her "kid" despite their age. Ok, it may sound a bit naff but unless you are a parent then you will never understand that. My son was very adept at saying so much in few words so I knew all along how he was and how life was treating him. His ups and downs. His highs and lows. And believe it or not, some fun situations. My emails to him were so long and so frequent I think he had matchsticks at the ready and a huge mug of coffee to keep awake when reading them.

Later Contact Problems And Why

Sometimes contact regarding girlfriends, boyfriends, partners, and spouses, can turn a little bit cool at some point. It's not you … honestly. It is not because they have gone off you either. It's because their life is so intensive that they can turn somewhat cold in their attitude. A coldness can be shown to everyone concerned. Life for them is hard and 24/7 they have to be especially careful and controlled in their day to day situations. Their romantic side tends to go down the drain now and again. So don't fret if that may happen on occasions.

Letters, emails and phone calls may become less frequent or even stop completely. It's an awful phase, but now you may understand the reason for this, ok. It can last weeks. It's just the mood swings that grab them at times. Like you they are upset and moody but that is something neither of you can see. One thinks the other can't be feeling as bad. So chin up and you will cope. The saying "You always hurt the one you love" can be spot on. It rears it's ugly head and it becomes another downer to deal with. No doubt some of your mail content out to them may be a little bit stilted even if you don't think so. It flows two ways. Mr. & Mrs. Trust are testing you both, for sure.

The Message You Wish You Had Never Sent!

Yep we all send at least one. The moment it is sent you regret it or after a night or two later and you have chewed things over about it in your mind you want to kick yourself for having even got so hung up about a minor thing you have made major. Oh to have Dr Who's time machine and to go back prevent you from ever having done it. So there it has gone to reach your loved one and give them a pretty sad time. I can't specifically say what that may be about as there are thousands of reasons the nasty one could have been written. Maybe because you think they don't want you now. It could be that you think they aren't replying to you as much or as lovingly as they did. Would it be blame, because the situation you are stuck in is all because of their career? The list is endless but whichever it is, there are no two ways about it, your emotions have boiled over. You got flaming mad and now you have Satan's horns coming out of your head. Oh hell, how horrible were your words? Hitting raw nerves from every angle. Now, you grit your teeth and inwardly hurt like mad for being such a "plonker" to have felt as bad as you did. Why, oh why did your anger have to be vented? It had to be, is why, because at that time you felt you might burst.

If they had been home you would have argued, as does everyone in life but you would have felt no deep lasting trauma about it. Then you would banter back and forth until a compromise or someone wins hands down. However, sending anger in message form is so hard to handle because until the person replies to it then the worry churns inside as to how the awful reaction is going to affect the next reply. How did your loved one take it? Would they consider you just had a bad day (not likely)? Would they think at all that it was a spur of the moment mistake? Another not likely. How is the venomous reply to it going to affect you? Oh no, will this mountain now cleverly made by you ever be overcome? Can the bridges be mended and resolved. Should you immediately contact them to say you didn't mean what you said? Desperately trying to explain that maybe it was a touch over the top even if you didn't think so at the time you wrote it. Would this "I am sorry" mail get there before the nasty one digs its claws in too deep?

It's going to take a lot of sweet mail to get things securely back on track. These things happen and none of us are perfect. Just know that most of the punishment you got from it was the emotions of regretting it ever left and that guilt complex. You opened the can of worms on yourself. Yes. For sure your error has hit you with worry right between your eyes.

So when the letter has to be written because you have no one to open up to who will understand what has just transpired between the two of you. DO NOT HIT SEND, I repeat DO NOT HIT SEND. Let it hang out in your drafts section if it's an email or just save it in quick letter writer, go pour a glass of wine or make a cup of tea and remember to breathe. Things will look better in the morning once the tempers have calmed and you will have saved yourself the heartache and possibly an ulcer from sending something that was written in the heat of the moment. If only we had our own personal "do not hit send police" waiting to help us out. It would save us a lot of stress in the end. Can you picture it, you've just written your very best, Nobel Prize winning, "How dare you, what were you thinking" letter. When your finger is hovering over the send button you all of a sudden could hear an electronic voice saying for you to step away from the computer, pull your hands away from the keyboard, please step away from the computer, as we are being handed a glass of virtual reality alcohol. This would then save you from stressing after having sent the letter and growing the most painful ulcer ever known to humankind. Always take into consideration that they may have a bad day and send you an unwanted message that has done exactly the same to them. They too will have opened that can of worms on themselves. Everything works both ways.

Reading Received Mail Over And Over Again

All people do this for smiles, joy and closeness. What a brilliant feeling it can bring. Time and time again you are thrilled to bits. So wow. It gives you boost after boost after boost, to enormously tingling inside levels. You may be sitting back in an armchair or even rereading it in bed. Ecstasy surrounds you every time. The words curl about you like an enormous hug. Each time you read it then it seems just as brilliant as when you first got it.

I have read. reread and read again my emails and cards that have been sent, to the point I'm sure I could recite each one off by heart. There are still days when I cry when I read them, but they lessen as the days move forward. For the most part I could light up a city in a black out, with how brightly I am glowing on the inside as I read the love he feels for me.

Reading Between The Lines

However beware. Be prepared. There can be times when some people go slightly bonkers and become negative. Silly to warn you because really it is something nobody can realise before hand but afterwards. It can do the opposite. You are maybe reading it on a very twisted "down" day. Oh dear me you can then read things between the lines. You pull each sentence apart and wonder if this sentence was meant to say what the words convey. Was it true or just written for your benefit? Then the next sentence and then the next until you think that the whole loving letter may be a sham. Then your "down" day is 100 times worse. Not too many people do this reading between the lines... thank heavens for that. A few do which is a big, big shame. This is Mr. & Mrs. Negative coming up to you. This is also Mr. & Mrs. Doubt creeping in too. Mr. & Mrs. Imagination hits you like a wet fish.

All have gripped you and made you feel so upset that you cannot deal with such thoughts. Eventually you will realise that you had your stupid head on when you dissected it. However, that is not until you have bawled your eyes out, paced up and down, felt angry and hurt that you go into horrific panic mode. You scream. You then begin to wonder what you may have done to make your loved one feel so anti you. Was it something you did? Was it something you said? Out come those tissues right from the start and you get through lots before the crying stops. Silliness can cause such enormous problems. Maybe, this warning may help you sort things out afterwards. Fingers crossed. All I can say is do not let your imagination go so wild that you turn loving mail into something opposite because on a bad hair day you decided to stupidly pull it apart and tried to read bad things into it. Love what they say and don't be a disbeliever.

Are Relationships Going Down Hill?

All this time apart is dreadful and soul destroying. It tests you both to an unbearable limit. You could end up finding a new partner and ditch your soldier. Out come the tissues. You may feel that coping with army life just isn't as simple as you thought. Not so clear-cut. Yes, you knew it wouldn't be a piece of cake but heavens you never thought it could be this hellish for you. Until your soldier went off to war then it all depends on your love for them as to your being able to fight your war at home. It's human nature after all and temptations can push you away from them. Managing to handle being apart is perhaps not working for you. There are so many emotional stresses so that bearing them can seem impossible. Depending on you, as a person, will be the choice whether you can ride this through or whether you just can't. Keep it in mind that your soldier has little to think about but life at home and doubts will traipse through your soldier's thoughts making them wonder if you might have found somebody else. It's only natural so don't be shocked by this. They will have seen a few people who's partner has fallen by the wayside in different ways so it worries them that they may end up the same as them. The next one on the list. The next to be jilted. Just face the fact that for some, having a soldier as a partner is just not on. It doesn't mean you are weak because you can't hack it. Think of it, as maybe the lifestyle doesn't suit you.

This time apart will certainly tell you for sure, one way or another. You just hope you get along fine, with no hitches. Also if you are positive enough to be reading this book then you probably are a person who wants to do what is best for you and your partner so that you know as much as you can to get you through the duration. The roller coaster and footy match. Think positive and ooze out those happy vibes. However, if things seem to have turned sour then such news of any jilting is best left until you see them face to face or on the phone. It doesn't go down too well in message form. Messages as shown above are very cruel. It is always best to be able to chat the problems through properly and fully together as to any reason you can't handle things regarding your love for each other. Isn't it ever going to be right or maybe a knee jerk reaction during an emotional time that perhaps can be put right? Until you talk it through then how can you make a fair judgment?

Why A Military Person? Ask My Friends And Family.

Let's face it, you are having a most terrible time and you don't like to be upset yourself by all of this questioning and facts stated by people who think they know best. However, you may have to jump to your soldier's defense and your own defense to explain to people that your loved one is worth all this hassle. Undoubtedly, people will ask you if it is really necessary to suffer all this heartbreak. Why did you get linked with a military person in the first place? Why didn't you find a love locally so to never suffer in this way? Lots of variations as to "Why did you?" Some

50

people will ask parents the "Why did your son or daughter join up in the first place if this is how it makes you feel?"

Love is an arrow that hits you and doesn't reckon as to that person's career. They are what they are and there is an end to it. As for parents they in no way can stop their son or daughter from choosing the lifestyle or job that they have set themselves. Free choice and all that jazz. So all these revelations will come at you from all sides making you think for some reason that perhaps you were an A1 twit to get stuck in this dilemma.

However, that is another part of the roller coaster of life you are involved with and no amount of people's questions will bring you to the ground. Be positive. When you answer all these irritating questions then don't back down. There will be lots of times when you even wonder yourself as to why you got involved in the very awesome life of military connections. Just keep in mind that all will be back to normal when your love returns. That's when all those annoying questions asked, go out of the window and are no longer relevant. Together once more. Your cheesy grin and elation will answer it in one. Of course it was worth the agony. A ghastly time that you both got through in different ways and you will both have come out the other side no matter what kicked you in the teeth along the way. And I know that I would not trade my man for anything in the world.

Children In The Situation

This part can only be brief, because each child can act so differently to all of this hassle. Attitudes can vary tremendously. There may be tantrums and tears when they are due to go to bed, or also the possibility of them starting to wet the bed during the night. There may be the same bad behaviour problems during the day. Tempers may be seen more often. All their rather "not so nice" character can be enhanced. The bottling up of emotions is another way. That can be when you think they are coping well yet they are not.

What child isn't going to miss having a parent away? Sadness will mingle through it. It is all a matter of degree. Children are much more resilient than people think they are. Children who have known military family lifestyle probably won't be as much affected by it as from day one they have known nothing else. Similarly all their friends will accept it.

Of course they are going to be saddened by not having a parent around. They are going to be yearning for them to be at home. They will pick up the not so good vibes and worries from their mum. It seems to rub off into the mix of things. Try to involve them in the parcels and it's contents so they feel a part of making dad happy while he's away missing them. Get them to choose a little gift to add to each parcel sent. Put in paintings they have done. If they are old enough, then get them to write their own letters to dad. Perhaps, dad could send them separate letters. Make them an equal part of the good things they can do. Participation is the key. Only you can work out the best way to handle this trying time throughout. Hopefully nothing will be too extreme.

A View From A Sister

Having a brother away can be hard, with all the strains and trials as all of us on this same roller coaster ride. However, different problems creep in sometimes. When a sister saw all of his friends safe and enjoying themselves and her brother away in such a ghastly, dangerous hell, far from home, it seemed so sad he wasn't amongst them. At the end of the day he had chosen the army and he was doing his job. She admired him for that and she knew she would enjoy watching him move up the ladder of promotion throughout his career. When he did phone and instant messenger her, it really would make her day and she would be jam packed with joy. There were sometimes the "down" ones. Then she worried herself sick especially if he phoned and for some reason she heard a little sadness in his voice or at least she sensed it. She wondered what trouble it could be. All our soldiers have low times. Scary times. Sometimes they have to un-bottle it to stay sane. Expect to have troubled calls at times or strange letters that hint slightly of anxiety.

When this sister saw her brother's girlfriend going out with someone else, it was the last straw. That threw her a real curve ball. She was then in a dilemma. Should she tell her brother or should she not mention it and let him find out on his return. She tossed and turned for days wondering which would be best. She wouldn't normally butt in to such things, but her brother was away totally blind to what was happening. Completely naïve to all of this. Every time she went out to the pub it hurt her to see this girlfriend with somebody else. In the end she decided her brother just had to be told so he wouldn't come home being the last person to know about this unfortunate event. After all, he had bigger worries in his life without this. There was no way she would allow her brother to be belittled as he would have been, if she hadn't said what was going on. It was a difficult thing to do and obviously his initial reaction was to be angry that she had told him.

The next day he apologised to her and was grateful she had been brave enough to let him know about it. He admitted he would have hated to return and be told by some friend. That proves that sometimes you have to be cruel to be kind. She had let the truth be unveiled to the brother she loved. So at all times in some way we have to become extremely protective to our soldier. We may have to make decisions as to which things are best for them to know and which are better unsaid. Only you can assess best how your loved one is likely to react to a problem. Only you can decide the best option. Many times we can feel we are struggling to know exactly what to say to them or if it is fair to say the not so good things. Our soldiers are not babies and don't have to be wrapped in cotton wool or protected against all the bumps in life. They may be in an unreal world that we can't understand so therefore some reality and truth can be given to them from our normal lives. At the end of the day you know what feels is the right thing to do. You know how they can handle certain things. A big responsibility on your shoulders. You know best if your soldier can handle certain news as each person is different. What one person can accept may be torture to another. So take care and think about it very carefully.

Compassionate Leave

Soldiers are allowed to come home for a short time if something untoward and urgent happens with direct relatives. It isn't for aunts or uncles or friends. It is for their wife, husband, children, parents or siblings. The army will decide on the amount of time they can be away. They may sometimes disapprove of some requests, so there are no cut and dry rules to this. The army does have a huge heart and of course they want their troops to be as much at ease as can be possible in such situations. The final decision is up to them as to whether or not the reason is valid.

It could be for a very serious or critical illness, so therefore it is essential they visit.

They may be about to be a dad so they are allowed home for the birth. They are usually allowed 2 weeks stay at this time. However first births are not compulsory and it is up to the regiment if they are allowed to come home, and second births depend on if you have friends and family close by. However, the main deciding factor is the operational environment that may not allow for them to have time away.

They may need to return for a funeral if it is a close family member or next of kin.

Every soldier is given a compassionate card which

the families can contact if they require their loved one home, this is a separate division from their regiment

Anything with a specific date like a wedding they want to go to then they have to have previously arranged for their R&R to be at that time or they may miss it.

R&R Dates (Rest And Recuperation). The Event That Seemed A Lifetime Away

Depending on how long they are out for will depend on how long or if they get R&R. Usually (and I use this term very loosely, very loosely) for a 6-month tour they will get 14 days. R&R starts the moment they step on the plane to return so you lose a day or so for time travelled. Dates will change (remember how the dates changed before they flew out) and time can be decreased, or (brace yourself) they aren't getting their R&R... It has been known to happen and it was something I experienced but such things do not happen frequently. Yes I know. Where is the justice in that? As we all have needs.

Depending on what is going on out there and depending on the jobs needed to be done will dictate when and how long they get for R&R. Due to operational environments planes and helicopters have designated flying hours and in some cases go over them to provide support to the troops who are fighting. They don't mind being delayed when it comes time for them to go back out but they hate being delayed when it comes time to fly home. They usually will find out the dates of when they get to come home for a break about a month and a half into the tour. This can vary though. You can expect them anywhere from close to the middle of their tour. Before or after it. Typically they like to come home in the middle as it breaks things up nicely, but who are we kidding, they don't get to pick when they come home for R&R.

My son had no choice because of things happening.

So at the time the soldiers were needed to remain for as long as possible. R&R was put on the back burner due to high alerts. Most either got their R&R reduced to a week and some got just a few days. Some got none at all. He was allowed five days. It was sad that his little daughter was only able to be with her dad for that meagre time. Out came those tissues. Such a disappointment for a little seven year old girl. Such a disappointment for his partner too.

My son was broken hearted with that and then he was faced with the fact that the army would make six monthers stay on for seven months. All because of it being a pretty rough time, but that's their job to do. Whatever is required of them. It was tragic that in seven months he only got home for five days. However, try to remember that this sort of thing is a rarity. I doubt you will ever suffer such an inhumane situation as that. Life for people who have loved ones at war, even when things go right it's a terrible struggle to manage. All we can do is be proud of them and make their life away as best as is possible and we at home have to fight our own battle of emotions. Day after day a new problem hits you in the face, so hang in there and think positive. By now, you will realise that negative attitudes get you nowhere do they?

Emotions When They Are Due To Arrive

Remember the emotional rollercoaster? Well its wheels are warming up again as the days get closer that they get to come home. You might as well buy shares in a tissue company because the amount that one goes through is amazing. There's our friend fright, anxiousness, excitement, all vying for positions at the front of the line and as they jostle and push each other out of the way, we find ourselves crying or short tempered because we are dealing with an emotional overload. And for the wives, husbands, partners, girlfriends and boyfriends we definitely forget to add the increased hormone activity with the excitement of releasing the pent up sexual frustration that really only gets satisfied with your soldier. (Sorry mum and dad but it had to be said).

All will count the days to the date of return. Ticking off the calendar. Oh for the time I can bin it. There is all this counting down in some form from the moment they leave to go to war. They also have their own countdown going on out there and are looking forward to coming home as we are to get them back. Throughout their career they are constantly counting down, for example what time will stag (guard watch) start and stop, how long till the next meal, and how long till the mail arrives. Clock watching for touchdown, which means yeah they are safe for sure even though it may be a short while. Big sighs of relief. For once you can breathe easier.

Picking Them Up At The Airport And Seeing Them

You can ask your loved one if you are allowed to pick them up at the airport (this will depend on their unit), usually for R&R you can but when they come home for good they may have to return back to their barracks with the military transport. Depending on where they are based will depend on where they will fly to. In order to get into the airport when you go to pick them up you will need their flight details. You can't be turning up at the wrong time. Dread the thought that you would be such a dilly.

You have to show two different sorts of proof of identification of yourself like a driving license and some identity too with a photo of yourself on it. Then all will be a "go" to be able to wrap your arms around them when you see them inside the airport. Equally, you may not be going to meet them and the first time you see them will be when they walk up to the front door. Either way it is a moment of great joy.

Not only are they excited to be coming home to you they are also worried for similar reasons. How will their R&R time work out? Of course it will be just perfect.

From the moment you get to hold them you both will get gooey eyed and won't want to let go or be out of each other's sight, the whole time. Here you are at last together once more even though this event seemed so far away and out of reach for such a long time. So you will enjoy every day to the full.

Some people (a very small minority) might find for a day or two that they're a bit standoffish or hanging out with the chaps too much and that you're starting to feel neglected. It's because they've developed a routine out there and the male company are all they've had for however long they've been gone so far. Even though you will be and are always there for them, no matter what, it can knock you back a bit. They don't want us to worry anymore than we do already with what they've seen over there. So the chaps moan with the other chaps to spare our feelings. Now, I know from our perspective we think, well that's insane. You would be able to handle anything that he has to get off his chest. He listens to you when you moan.

If you don't understand why he feels that you wouldn't be able to handle it, it's not that you wouldn't be able to handle it. They want to keep us safe from having to hear what it is that they have seen and experienced. From the media, you only see a minute amount of what is really going on out there. To hear all of it and see the pain in their eyes would be tough no matter how you look at it. So it's not because they love you any less but it's because they are deeply in love with you and there's some things you just don't need to know. And before you know it they will have got it all worked out of their system and they will soon be thinking, chaps... What chaps? I just want to hang out with my lass and not let her go. That's why he wanted to be home. Just for you in as many ways as possible.

For the lady soldier she just wants to be with her chap and be in his arms. She feels the same way as the men but I doubt if she will want to be off "pubbing it" alone in the first few days but she will be just as reticent when it comes to talking about the things she has seen and done and she wont want to talk about those. Just as likely is they are returning home to mum and dad or family but whoever you are don't try to ask them deep questions. They haven't come home to give you that sort of information. They have returned to get a lovely break with their minds completely off the subject. They want to have R&R as a state for safety and normality. A time to relax and have fun. Bliss is what they crave for.

So make the most of your time together in the way that fits you best. Go out or stay home or do a mix of both. At last you have precious freedom to do whatever you want to. Doesn't time fly, though? It always does when it's something good. It certainly isn't a time to spend dashing round to see all relatives in this so short period. Take things easy, enjoy and chill out. They haven't had that opportunity for months. It's so very important. They need a very restful time indeed.

R&R Is Over

Then the emotional rollercoaster comes to the gate once again when it's time for them to go back. Those two weeks only seemed like one week, if that. It seems harder the second time to say good-bye, and soon you stop saying good-bye and replace it with see you later or talk to you soon so this way it never seems final. The mantra starts up "I will not cry when they leave, I will not cry when they leave." And you could secretly wish, oh dread the thought, they hadn't come home for R&R because you had just gotten used to them being gone and now you have to start the process all over again. Oh heavens you are both back to square 1. But who are we kidding? You were chuffed to bits that they were home. The time was golden. You wouldn't have missed it for the world. Despite the special time had, the pain seems greater when they have to return. You do know that when they will be coming home again when their tour is over then it's for good. Yippee, just imagine that. The time until that happens is getting closer and closer but seems to be miles off. You dealt with the first half so somehow you will deal with the last half.

The Last And Final Countdown

The days seem to slowly start to move forward with you wondering if the day will ever come that they will be back home. Everyday is a crawl. A huge ache. Eventually without warning, you look at the calendar and something clicks and you hear that voice in your head let out a whoop of joy of "OH MY GAWD THEY ARE HOME IN ONLY 3 WEEKS!!!!!!!!!!!!!!!!!!!!" There's a happy dance of hyper elation plus a few tears of excitement (guess we'll still need those tissues) of realising that your loved one, that you've missed more than anything you ever thought possible, is going to be home in a few short weeks. Now the "pull out all stops planning" comes into play. I have to go grocery shopping to get all the ingredients to make his favourite meal. Baking or ordering a special cake which can be as simple as "Welcome Home" or a specific design such as a tank, plane or paratrooper landing site complete with it's own landed toy paratroopers. What am I going to wear on the day he comes home (like that really matters), as you survey your closet you can't find anything to wear, which is similar to standing in front of a fully stocked fridge and thinking there's nothing to eat.

This only means one thing you must go shopping

for something new to wear, oh darn it. That will be a chore! Decorating the house up with banners, balloons and other decorations upon their return. They have to be bought too. Creating a romantic boudoir effect in the bedroom, which can include sheer fabric in reds or oranges, draped over the bedside table lampshades to cast a romantic glow in the room (this can be safer than using candles). Silk rose petals to be scattered on top of the bed. If you have a wrought iron head board or one that isn't solid wood you can weave twinkle lights throughout the head board to create a romantic look. You can get what's called a lamp ring and they are made out of terra cotta or ceramic and they are placed on top of the light bulb with a couple of drops of fragrant oils and the heat from the bulb will make the room smell nice and romantic. There could be finishing the final plans on the vacation the two of you are taking together after they return. Everything has to be perfect for when they come home for good and it seems like just yesterday you said your goodbyes when they first left for the start of their tour!! And yesterday and yesterday and yesterday.... So many yesterdays.

Pacing. Oh my goodness I can't stop pacing. The house is all clean and I'm sure there is a shine to the walls. My nerves are shot. I can't believe that it is just around the corner that he's coming home!! My new outfit is bought. The house is prepared. I've even worn my new outfit around the house because I like it so much to give it a test run for the big day making sure to stop in front of every mirror in the house to make sure I still look okay after leaving the last room. Practicing the odd pose or two for effect. I've done all the washing and am ready to do one final load of sheets on the day he comes home so when we crawl into bed he has fresh clean sheets to snuggle between without any sand. I think my butterflies must have been taking steroids because they are way bigger and more active than ever before and I feel like a giggly little schoolgirl about to go out on her first date. I'm so glad that I've made a hair appointment because I really don't think I could manage to get it looking normal with the excitement level that is coursing through my veins right now. I'm pretty sure it would be off the charts if it could be measured. I never thought this day would come six months ago but then I think dare I really believe that six months has passed. Time has gone so slowly that it hurt with each hour. Now it's all turned around thank goodness.

Decompression

When their tour has been overly eventful and stressful for them, they make a 24-hour pit stop before coming home. This is usually done in Cyprus where they can enjoy plenty of beers, a grand barbque, and water sports. Oh and lets not forget allowing them to act purely like rowdy boys without having to worry about getting in trouble for their behaviour. This little stop over allows them to blow off the steam of what they've been through over the course of their tour so when they then get on the flight to come home to us they are refreshed and revitalized and can then concentrate on being back home. Soldiers always have counsellors available if they need them once they are back. Balancing things out is essential and some need more help than others to put things in a better perspective.

They get to talk to a priest, psychiatrist, and counsellor before coming home. However, one day does not allow to fully blow off stress, anxiety, loss and grief. Throughout the tour the support from home is great and much appreciated, but just remember the environments, temper, outrage, and the needing of ones own space is also required along with continued support from loved ones and family members is most needed when they return home. They know that things have changed while they've been away but we must also remember that they've changed as well with what they've experienced out there. So just give them time to adjust to being back and the surroundings of everything and all will be fine. Being away so many months it will be noticed that people have new routines now which have come about with family. Children sprout up so quickly and have probably now got different attitudes as in that time they have blossomed and grown. A baby they leave behind may now be weaned or have taken their first steps. An older child may have started school. All these things they have missed. So many things that naturally you have watched happening gradually. All of a sudden the soldier gets zapped in the face to see immediately. Many differences to take on board and a lot to become accustomed to. Coming home is no easy time. It is hard work to come to terms with and get their head round. Patience and understanding is required until all is settled and calm. It takes time, but all will get back to normal fairly soon. So smile as it will all fall into place.

My soldier's home safe now the tour is completed. HURRAY!

The day comes when at last the tour is finished and done with and normality will reign. Ecstasy at last. Your dream has come true. What a relief. Phew. You can breathe again. Nobody can realise how you both are feeling. All the hassle is behind you. No more counting off the months, weeks, days and hours to this time. Yipeeeeeeee. You wowed them at the airport or the moment your loved one walked through the door. They probably will cause you to stare at them and your jaw could fall open as you see the fantastic tan they now have. Perhaps you forgot about that. That practice with your hair and make-up just knocks them off their feet. It was so worthwhile. Any D.I.Y you did will take their breath away when they see what you have done.

Now no more roller coaster to ride, no desperation waiting for a phone call, no more mail or parcels to send or other means of limited contact that has blighted the situation. No more worries of the dangerous things that whizzed around in your heads. No more wild imaginings that constantly possessed you. No avoiding the TV news or newspapers. You can put away every torment. No having to see them go back like in R&R. As for those tissues constantly at your side then they can go take a hike. That tatty worn out calendar can go in the bin. Such heaven it is now that everything is back on track. The clock is at normal speed. Negatives are now positives. You are overwhelmed.

Here you are glued to each other. Life will be as it was before you were separated. A few phone calls to friends and relatives to give them the good news wouldn't go amiss. The only thing you both have to sort is reversing the list of things that had to be done before they left. Get the bills right and get the car back on the road. Perhaps that car needs a service with all that standing about. Your soldier may be a bit touched with jet lag but that's nothing to worry about. The body clock will soon sort itself out. Home, home, home. How much better can it be? You both went through an emotional living hell but you got through to the other side. You both survived it all even if it was unbelievably hard. Be proud that yes you sure did it. Maybe you deserve a medal for your battle. Triumphant. If you got through that then you can cope with most things life may fling at you in the future.

Epilogue

When I started the six month countdown I thought that the days would never end and time would drag its feet. It seemed like all of a sudden, the little fairy in charge of time waved her magic wand at last and it was time for him to come home. I'll never forget the emotional rollercoaster throughout this experience and I'll cherish all of the great friends I've made from the ebluey chatboard. Without their support this tour would've been much more difficult. It seems that once you get the first tour under your belt, the training wheels come off and you've now become a pro on how to handle them gone. Although I can't guarantee that the emotional rollercoaster gets any easier and the amount that you miss them will always be the same.

Our words of advice still stand and always remember "no news is good news." They miss us just as much as we miss them and they can't wait to come home to us. Have fun with all your new and exciting projects you start while they are away and by keeping busy the time passes by much more quickly. As each and every day passes you are one day closer to your loved one coming home.

May they stay safe and strong to return to your loving arms and they will always be within our thoughts and prayers.

Printed in the United Kingdom
by Lightning Source UK Ltd.
134259UK00001B/100/A